Contents

Lady Gaga   4

Dizzee Rascal   6

Rihanna   8

Justin Bieber   10

Beyoncé   12

Jason Derülo   14

Pixie Lott   16

Jay-Z   18

Miley Cyrus   20

Other Pop Stars   22

More stars to look out for   24

Index   24

Lady Gaga

THE ECCENTRIC STAR

Lady Gaga in Berlin in 2009, launching new headphones in collaboration with hip-hop artist Dre.

Lady Gaga loves the music of David Bowie and Madonna. Glam-rock band Queen's hit single *Radio Gaga* inspired her unusual stage name.

Stats!

Name: Stefani Joanne Angelina Germanotta

Date of birth: 28 March 1986

First hit: In 2008 Lady Gaga stormed to the top of the charts in the USA, UK, Australia, Canada and Ireland with her first single *Just Dance*.

Albums: *The Fame* (2008), *The Fame Monster* (2009).

Career highlights: Lady Gaga notched up two Grammy awards in 2010 with the award for Best Electronic/Dance Album for her debut album *The Fame* and Best Dance Recording for *Poker Face*. She also won three Brit Awards for Best International Album, International Solo Artist and International Breakthrough Act. The NME gave her awards for both Best Dressed and Worst Dressed act of 2010!

Personal life: Touring, dreaming up new and exciting performances and working on new material takes up most of Lady Gaga's time. She claims she was in love once but her boyfriend didn't want her to be a singer.

Secrets of success: Lady Gaga is a walking work of art. She is also a talented musician and songwriter. She's written for Britney Spears, Fergie and Justin Timberlake.

PO   RS

LIZ GOGERLY

Published in 2013 by Wayland

Copyright © Wayland 2013

Wayland
338 Euston Road
London NW1 3BH

Wayland Australia
Level 17/207 Kent Street
Sydney, NSW 2000

Senior editor: Camilla Lloyd
Designer: Stephen Prosser

Picture Acknowledgments: The author and publisher would like to thank the following for allowing their pictures to be reproduced in this publication: Cover and 4: Action Press/Rex Features; Angela Weiss/Getty Images: 14; Rex Features: 5, 16; Brian Rasic/Rex Features: 6, 7, 10; Startraks Photo/Rex Features: 9; BDG/Rex Features: 11; Sipa Press/Rex Features: 13, 18, 22 (bottom), 23 (bottom); NBCU Photobank/Rex Features: 15; Jonathan Hordle/Rex Features: 17; Matt Baron/BEI/Rex Features: 22 (top); Gregory Pace/BEI/Rex Features: 23 (top); Gustavo Miguel Fernandes/Shutterstock: 1 and 21; Stocklight/Shutterstock: 2 and 8; Cinemafestival/Shutterstock: 12, 22 (middle); Adam Gasson/Shutterstock: 19; Dooley Productions/Shutterstock: 20; iladam/Shutterstock: 23 (middle); LoopAll/Shutterstock: 24.

British Library Cataloguing in Publication Data:
Gogerly, Liz.
Pop stars. – (Celebrity secrets)
1. Rock musicians–Biography–Juvenile literature.
I. Title II. Series
782.4'2166'0922-dc22

ISBN: 978 0 7502 7153 0

Printed in China

Wayland is a division of Hachette Children's Books, an Hachette UK company.

www.hachette.co.uk

Life Story

Lady Gaga blows audiences away with her wild fashions and innovative shows. At Glastonbury in 2009 she wore a dress made from plastic bubbles. On *The X-Factor* she performed on a piano in a sink while sitting on a toilet! Lady Gaga's crazy make-up and wigs always cause a stir.

Stefani Germanotta was born and raised in New York by her Italian-American parents. She has a younger sister, Natali. Lady Gaga learned to play the piano when she was four and wrote her first song at 13. At 17 she attended the Tisch School of Arts at New York University. She left in her second year to concentrate on her music.

Success did not come overnight for Lady Gaga. She was dropped by Def Jam Records after only three months. She went on to form a band and write songs for other artists. Eventually Lady Gaga signed with Akon's record label and broke into the charts with her debut album *The Fame*. The Gaga phenomenon went global with number one singles *Just Dance* and *Poker Face*.

Lady Gaga loves fashion and puts together some wild stage outfits.

The Fame Monster (2009) and *Born this Way* (2011) have been two of her hugely successful albums.

Lady Gaga tours extensively and adores her fans – she calls them 'little monsters'. Despite rumours of illness and exhaustion, the new princess of pop just keeps on going.

Questions and Answers

Q What is your musical goal?

A "My true legacy will be the test of time, and whether I can sustain a space in pop culture and really make stuff that will have a genuine impact."

Lady Gaga, *Rolling Stone*, May 2009

Q What do you spend your money on?

A "You see, I don't really spend money and I don't really like fame. I spend my money on my shows – but I don't like buying things. I don't buy diamonds…I'll spend it on fashion."

Lady Gaga, *The Sunday Times*, May 2010

Dizzee Rascal

BRITISH RAP SUPERSTAR

Dizzee Rascal after winning the Mercury Prize in 2010.

Stats!

Name: Dylan Kwabena Mills

Date of birth: 1 October 1985

First hit: Dizzee had already notched up four top-20 hits before his number one hit *Dance Wiv Me* in 2008.

Albums: His debut album *Boy in da Corner* (2003) was a top-30 hit. His subsequent three albums *Showtime* (2004), *Maths + English* (2007) and *Tongue N' Cheek* (2009) have all been top-ten hits in the UK.

Career highlights: He became the first male rapper to win the Mercury Prize with his first album *Boy in da Corner* in 2003. He scooped the NME Award for Innovation in 2004 and two Brit Awards in 2010 for Best British Male and Best International Act. He also performed at the London 2012 Olympic Games Opening Ceremony!

Personal life: Dizzee was devastated in 2008 when his ex-girlfriend was killed in a motorway car crash.

Secrets of success: Dizzee's achievements are down to putting all his energy into his music and believing in himself.

At school Dizzee was always in trouble. When one of his old teachers called him Rascal, the name stuck!

Life Story

In June 2010 Dizzee Rascal was one of the main acts at the Glastonbury Festival. Everyone in the crowd knew the words to his hit *Bonkers*. Later Dizzee was joined by Florence Welch (of Florence and the Machine) for *You've Got the Dirtee Love*. Then the crowd went bonkers! Less than a decade earlier it would have been impossible to predict that Dizzee would cause such excitement.

Questions and Answers

Q **What would have happened to you if you hadn't found music?**

A "I'd have just ended up carrying on a life of crime, I suppose. Where I'm from, there ain't a lot of other options, you know what I'm saying? Entertainment or football or crime. I don't want to spread the message that all you can do is music or sport. You can be anything. Anything. That's the message I like to spread."

Dizzee Rascal, the *Guardian*, September 2003

Q **How did writing help you get through the tough years on the street?**

A "I could be at one with myself, get into a zone, and then create something. I loved that feeling. That buzz was more addictive to me than anything on the planet."

Dizzee Rascal, the *Observer*, September 2009

Dizzee Rascal performed with Lily Allen at the O2 Arena in March 2010.

Dylan Mills, aka Dizzee Rascal, shot to fame aged 18 in 2003 but it could have been very different. Dizzee's father died when he was young. He was raised by his mother on a council estate in east London. Dizzee grew up quickly, but was often in trouble at school. He was excluded from school four times, but when he found music, it gave him something to focus on.

Dizzee's early lyrics were about life on the streets. He wrote about the poverty, gun crime and isolation that black kids often feel. He fused different styles of music such as garage, hip-hop and even rock. The result was something so original it was given a new name – grime! Dizzee's first albums were full of anger. More recently he's been having fun and it shows in his music. He's the UK's favourite rap star.

Rihanna

GOOD GIRL GONE BAD?

Rihanna at an awards ceremony in Hollywood.

At school Rihanna reckons she was a real nerd. If she wasn't a singer she thinks she would have been a psychologist.

Stats!

Name: Robyn Rihanna Fenty

Date of birth: 20 February 1988

First hit: In 2005 Rihanna had a dancehall hit with *Pon De Replay*.

Albums: Rihanna's debut album *Music of the Sun* (2005) was a top-ten hit in the USA. Her third album *Good Girl Gone Bad* (2007) was a number one hit in the UK and reached number two in the USA. *Rated R*, released in 2009 was a top-ten hit in both the USA and the UK. Both *Loud* (2010) and *Talk that Talk* (2011) have been album successes for the Barbadian singer.

Career highlights: In the summer of 2007 everyone everywhere was singing along to Rihanna's single *Umbrella*. It reached number one in 27 countries. *Umbrella* also stayed at the top of the UK charts for ten weeks, making it the longest running number one hit of the decade.

Personal life: Rihanna's previous relationship with singer Chris Brown ended when he physically assaulted her. Rihanna hopes that other young women can gain strength from what happened to her and leave a harmful relationship.

Secrets of success: Rihanna can sing and dance. She has also created a great image for herself. She has a cool haircut and wears stylish clothes and stage costumes.

Life Story

Rihanna returned home to Barbados to celebrate her 20th birthday in 2008. The whole island partied and celebrated its first 'Rihanna Day'! The islanders are proud of Rihanna and her international stardom.

Rihanna grew up in Saint Michael, Barbados. She always wanted to sing. Rihanna had a troubled childhood. Her father was a drug addict and her parents eventually split up. Rihanna was often left in charge of her three younger brothers. She was forced to grow up quickly. She believes this has given her the strength to cope with her sudden fame and media attention.

Stardom came quickly to Rihanna at a young age. She was 16 when music producer Evan Rogers watched her audition. Before long Rihanna was off to New York to record a demo. Then came a meeting with the record producer, Jay-Z. Within a week of that meeting she was signed to his Def Jam record label.

Rihanna shows off her stylish image at a concert in Florida in 2010.

Rihanna's debut album *Music of the Sun* is a fusion of reggae, R 'n' B and soca (West Indian soul calypso). Less than a year later came the hit album *A Girl Like Me* with its number one single *SOS*. In 2007 she created a sexy new look and a different sound. Still a teenager, she released her most successful album to date, *The Girl Gone Bad*. The mega hit *Umbrella* made her an international star.

Questions and Answers

Q How did you feel about the success of *Umbrella*?

A "I never knew that this song was going to be so big. And I still can't really fathom how big it blew up to become, in places all over this world that I've never heard of. I couldn't really get a hold of that. To this day it never gets old. It's a magical song to me."

Rihanna, *CBS News*, 2009

Q Do you think fame has changed you like it has some other stars?

A "People really thought I was going to get out of my head and become some super diva chick. And to this day that never happened. I don't ask for extravagant things like flowers flown in, or the room to be all one colour."

Rihanna, the *Guardian*, May 2008

Justin Bieber

TEEN POP IDOL

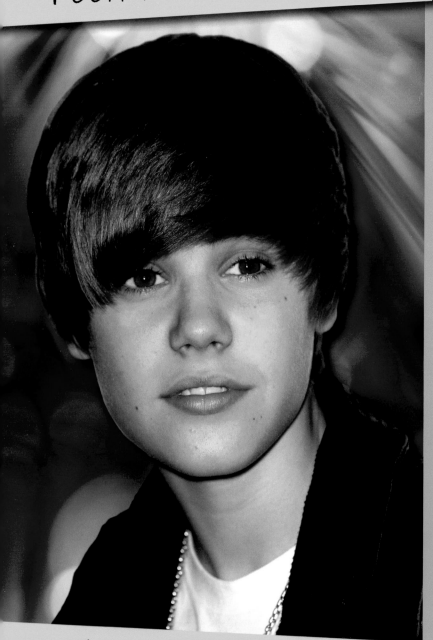

Justin Bieber performed at the Capital FM Summertime Ball in 2010.

Stats!

Name: Justin Drew Bieber

Date of birth: 1 March 1994

First hit: *One Time* released in 2009 was a hit in more than ten countries.

Albums: Justin's album *My World* was released in 2009. It reached number one in Canada and was a top-ten hit in the UK and the USA.

Career highlights: Justin is the first new artist to have seven songs from a debut album reach the *Billboard Hot 100* (the US charts that are published each week in *Billboard* magazine).

Personal life: Cute and good looking, Justin could take his pick of girls. He's been dating since he was 13. His last serious girlfriend was Caitlin Beadles. At the time of going to press the romance with Caitlin is back on…

Secrets of success: Justin is a talented singer and he also taught himself to play the guitar, piano, trumpet and drums.

Justin performed for President Barack Obama at the White House for a special Christmas concert in December 2009.

Life Story

In 2009 'Bieber Fever' hit the world. These days the teenage singer can no longer walk down the street without being mobbed. Girls think he's cute, yet behind that fresh face and mop of hair is a talented singer and songwriter.

Justin was born in Stratford, Ontario in Canada. His parents divorced when he was young (he writes about the divorce in his song *Down to Earth*). He was interested in playing music from the age of two! At 12 he entered a singing competition in Stratford. Justin didn't win, but soon after his mother began uploading his first performances onto YouTube. At the time Justin was mostly doing covers of his favourite songs.

Scott Braun, a music manager, watched one of Justin's videos by accident and was hugely impressed by him.

In a matter of months Scott had persuaded Justin and his mother to come to Atlanta to do some demo tracks. Next came a meeting with Justin's hero, the superstar Usher.

The King of R'n'B was impressed enough to sign Justin to Island Records, his record company. Usher has helped to manage Justin's career ever since.

The future looks bright for Justin Bieber. His first album *My World* has gone platinum in Canada, the USA and the UK. In 2010 he began his first world tour. But, however big he gets, Justin stays true to his original fans. He still uploads videos onto YouTube and fans can follow his every move on Twitter.

Questions and Answers

Q So why do you do what you do?

A "I want them [girls] to hear my music and wanna play it again because it made their hearts feel good."

Q Who do you look up to?

A "Usher, he's who I want to model my career on."

Justin Beiber, interview, April 2010 (both quotes above)

Q Do you ever find it all too much?

A "I don't really get nervous. Ever since I was little I've liked being the centre of attention."

Justin Bieber, the *Observer*, April 2010

Justin performs in 2010.

Beyoncé

QUEEN OF R'N'B

Beyoncé at the Cannes Film Festival in France.

Stats!

Name: Beyoncé Giselle Knowles

Date of birth: 4 September 1981

First hit: Beyoncé was part of the successful girl group Destiny's Child. Her solo career took off in 2003 with *Crazy in Love* reaching number one in the USA and the UK.

Albums: In 2003 Beyoncé's debut solo album *Dangerously in Love* was number one in the UK and the USA. *I Am… Sasha Fierce* (2008) was another number one in the USA and reached number two in the UK.

Career highlights: Singing for President Obama and his wife Michelle's first dance as President and First Lady of America. She was so nervous before the performance that she cried.

Personal life: Beyoncé is 'Dangerously in Love' with husband Jay-Z, and gave birth to daughter Blue Ivy Carter in January 2012.

Secrets of success: On stage she is sexy and energetic. In real life she's shy and polite and very likeable.

Beyoncé and her mother Tina Knowles launched their own fashion line the House of Deréon in 2006.

Life Story

Beyoncé is beyond pop stardom. In 2010 she was named the second most powerful celebrity in the world by *Forbes* magazine. She's sold more than 100 million records as a solo artist and as a member of Destiny's Child. In 2008 she won six Grammy Awards in one night – a first for any female performer. Lead roles in films like *Dreamgirls* (2006) and *Cadillac Records* (2008) show she has what it takes to succeed in Hollywood, too.

Beyoncé in concert in Brazil in 2010.

Beyoncé was born in Houston, Texas. Part of Beyoncé's appeal is her magnificent stage presence and dazzling costumes. However, as a young girl she was shy, but she had the ability to sing. This was discovered when she won a school talent show. At eight she joined the band Girl's Tyme. In 1993 they became Destiny's Child.

Hits like *Survivor* and *Bootylicious* brought them masses of fans.

In 2003 Beyoncé went solo with the album *Dangerously In Love*. Destiny's Child split up in 2005. By then Beyoncé's film career was taking off, too.

In 2008 *I Am... Sasha Fierce* was another hit. She claims Sasha is her on-stage persona. As Sasha she can be the wild and wonderful pop diva we know and love. The rest of the time she is 'B' – the hard-working, polite and dedicated star we admire.

Questions and Answers

Q **What does it take to succeed in the pop business?**

A "It takes discipline, and it takes focus and I think I'm very fortunate that I've had gradual success. It's not something that happened in one day. It's something I've worked at and worked at."

Beyoncé, *CBS News*, 2009

Q **Do you feel that you've paved the way for more black women to achieve world success?**

A "I am really proud that I am one of the artists that has the opportunity to be on magazine covers and to be in the movies. And I do think that I'm opening doors for more black women, just like Halle [Berry] and Diana Ross opened doors for me."

Beyoncé, *Marie Claire*, September 2008

Jason Derülo

Jason Derülo in Los Angeles in 2010.

Stats!

Name: Jason Joel Desrouleaux

Date of birth: 21 September 1989

First hit: Jason's first single *Whatcha Say* was a hit in 2009, reaching number one in the USA and number three in the UK.

Albums: Jason released his debut album *Jason Derülo* in 2010. It peaked at number 11 in the USA and number eight in the UK.

Career highlights: In 2009–2010 Jason hit the road with Lady Gaga on her sensational *The Monster Ball Tour*. To date, Jason claims that being in front of thousands and thousands of fans each day is the most amazing experience of his career.

Personal life: At the moment there's nobody special in Jason's life. He has said he'd like to meet somebody like his mum – someone with a big heart who's honest!

Secrets of success: He's totally focused on music. Jason is also versatile and is inspired by everything from classical music and rock to hip-hop. He doesn't want his music to be placed in a particular genre.

Jason is religious and prays everyday. He believes that having faith gives him the confidence in his life.

Life Story

Jason Derülo has exploded onto the music scene. With a smash hit debut single and album he is one of the biggest breakthrough acts of 2010.

Jason was born in Miami, Florida to Haitian-American parents. Nobody in the family was musical but Jason always loved music. He was eight when he wrote his first song about his crush on a girl called Amy. At family get-togethers he was always the one dancing and singing. His parents had good jobs and were able to afford performing arts classes. Jason studied theatre, opera and ballet in Florida. He then graduated from the American Musical and Dramatic Academy in New York.

Studying a broad spectrum of performing arts has helped to shape his music. At 16 he was already writing songs for big acts such as P. Diddy and Sean Kingston.

Questions and Answers

Q How do you feel about becoming famous?

A "I just make music and at the end of the day I just hope that the world receives me. I don't want to make music for a small amount of people, I want the maximum amount of people to be affected by it. Music really heals the world, and I would love to be the biggest healer."

Jason Derülo, *beatweek* magazine, March 2010

Q How would you describe your first album?

A "You can expect reinvention – a record full of surprises... I have pop/rock songs on there; I have big ballads; I have club records that make you dance... So however you're feeling, there's a song on the album that can mirror it."

Jason Derülo, *Blues & Soul* magazine, August 2010

Jason always knew that he wanted to be the one at the front of the stage performing. He was finally signed to Warner Brother Records and Beluga Heights Records in 2007. His debut single *Whatcha Say* in 2009 was a massive hit. *In My Head, Ridin' Solo* and *What If* have charted in the top ten.

Jason strongly believes in the healing power of music. He reckons everything is possible with hard work and dedication. In person he is polite and softly spoken. In an interview in 2010 he said: "A lot of my dreams have come true and I'm happy because I get to do what I love every day."

Jason performs on the Tonight Show with Jay Leno in May 2010.

Pixie Lott

RISING STAR OF POP

Pixie attends a film premiere in 2010.

Stats!

Name: Victoria Louise Lott

Date of birth: 12 January 1991

First hit: Pixie's first single *Mama Do (Uh Oh, Uh Oh)* went straight to number one in the UK in June 2009.

Albums: *Turn it Up* was released in September 2009 and it reached number six in the UK Album charts.

Career highlights: Pixie loved her time at Italia Conti Academy of Theatre Arts: She has said about her time at Italia Conti: "It was the best days of my life so far … it's just full of life and there's never a dull moment."

Personal life: Pixie hasn't had a serious boyfriend yet.

Secrets of success: How does Pixie write about love and heartache so convincingly when she hasn't fallen in love? She says she writes songs in the heat of the moment. If she's had an argument with somebody or is feeling happy about something, she writes. This helps her get into the character of a song.

Pixie's music heroes include Mariah Carey, Britney Spears and Lady Gaga. She also likes Kings of Leon.

Life Story

Pixie Lott has packed a lot into her young life. By the age of 18 she had a major record deal, a best-selling album, two number one singles and two MTV awards. Next she starred in *Fred: The Movie*. What will this talented young girl from Essex do next?

Pixie was born in Bromley, south east London. She was a tiny baby so her mother nicknamed her Pixie. In interviews Pixie claims she began singing in the cot. At five she was attending singing, dancing and acting classes. When she was 11 her dream of going to drama school came true. She was awarded a scholarship to study at London's famous Italia Conti Academy. At 12 she made her London stage debut in *Chitty Chitty Bang Bang* as one of the sewer children.

Pixie performs at T4 on the Beach in 2010.

Pixie always wanted to be a pop star. She was 14 when she saw the ad: 'Looking for the Next Hot Diva'. Manager David Sonenberg was looking for girls aged over 16 so Pixie lied about her age.

David was so impressed with her voice he became her manager. Pixie's career took off quickly. She was signed up by Island Def Music Group in the USA. She was still at school but successfully juggled her music career and work.

In 2007 she was snapped up by British label Mercury. Then in 2009 she burst onto the scene with her number one hit *Mama Do (Uh Oh, Uh Oh)*. Pixie has had a quick rise to the top and she intends to stay there.

Questions and Answers

Q What was it like when you first got into the music business?

A "One day I'd be out in LA recording songs, the next day I'd be back at school doing GCSE maths. And I wouldn't tell anyone about it, in case it didn't happen."

Pixie Lott, *Daily Mail*, June 2009

Q Did you ever think you wouldn't make it as a pop star?

A " I just went for every opportunity and I thought that if I kept going, it would happen. No. I always had the determination. I couldn't imagine not doing what I wanted to do."

Pixie Lott, the *Guardian*, June 2010

Jay-Z

THE KING OF RAP

Jay-Z attends the premiere of hit movie *American Gangster*.

Stats!

Name: Shawn Corey Carter

Date of birth: 4 December 1969

First hit: Jay-Z has released over 40 singles. In 2009 he finally got his first number one hit in the USA with *Empire State of Mind* (featuring Alicia Keys). *Run This Town* (2009) was a number one in the UK.

Albums: Jay-Z hit the top 30 in the USA in 1996 with his classic debut album *Reasonable Doubt*. He's made 11 studio albums and four collaboration albums.

Career highlights: Jay-Z doesn't like award ceremonies but he's certainly picked up a few awards. He's won ten Grammy Awards and the Brit Award for Best International Male Solo Artist in 2010.

Personal life: He married fellow R'n'B star Beyoncé Knowles in 2008, who gave birth to their daughter Blue Ivy Carter in 2012.

Secrets of success: He has had a longer career in the business than any other rap artist. As well as a wonderful way with words, Jay-Z has never been afraid to take risks and try something different.

Jay-Z hobnobs with Presidents (Obama and Clinton!) and counts Ralph Fiennes, Gwyneth Paltrow and Chris Martin as friends.

Life Story

In 2009 Jay-Z hit 40 and had plenty of reasons to celebrate. He's one of the leading rappers in the world having sold over 40 million albums worldwide. He's also a top businessman with interests outside the music business including clothing lines and sports clubs.

Questions and Answers

Q What is rap music?

A "Rap for me is like making movies, telling stories, and getting the emotions of the songs through in just as deep a way."

Jay-Z, *Interview* magazine, January 2010

Q What is it like being famous?

A "I have a gift and with that gift certain things come with it. You have to put up with people who think of you this way and people who think of you that way. And put up with not ever having a moment to chill or relax if you're outside."

Jay-Z to MTV, November 2002

Jay-Z has come a long way from Brooklyn, New York where he was born and raised. When his father walked out, his mother was left to bring up a young family. It was his mum who bought him a boom box and first got him into making music. Known as Jazzy by his mates (which is where he gets the name Jay-Z), he began making records in the 1980s. In those days he was tall, skinny and famous for wearing one leg of his sweat pants rolled up above his knee. He was also no stranger to violence and getting into scrapes with rivals on the rap scene.

Major labels didn't want to sign him but in 1996 Jay-Z began to make his mark. He helped to set up the independent label Roc-A-Fella-Records. Soon after he released his classic debut *Reasonable Doubt*. Since then Jay-Z has had 11 number one albums in the USA, breaking the record once held by the King of rock 'n' roll Elvis. Once upon a time Jay-Z was a cult underground rapper. Now he can be credited with helping to bring rap music into the mainstream.

Jay-Z performs at Glastonbury, 2008.

Miley Cyrus

POPSTAR AND MOVIE STAR

Miley attends the City for Hope Concert in Los Angeles.

When Miley was a little girl her father always called her 'Smiley'. Later this was shortened to Miley. In 2008, she officially changed her name from Destiny Hope to Miley Ray.

Stats!

Name: Destiny Hope Cyrus

Date of birth: 23 November 1992

First hit: *Party in the USA* (2009) was number two in the USA and number three in the UK, making it her most successful single to date.

Albums: Miley's three studio albums are *Meet Miley Cyrus* (2007), *Breakout* (2008) and *Can't Be Tamed* (2010). She's also recorded two live albums and two soundtracks: *Hannah Montana: The Movie* (2009) and *The Last Song: Original Soundtrack* (2010).

Career highlights: She was catapulted to stardom playing Miley Stewart/Hannah Montana in the Disney sitcom *Hannah Montana*. She auditioned for the part when she was 11 but had to wait two years before she got it.

Personal life: Miley dated Nick Jonas for two years, they broke up at the end of 2007. At 15 Miley dated model Justin Gaston. Miley also dated Australian actor Liam Hemsworth making the romantic movie *The Last Song*. They split up in 2010.

Secrets of success: Fans adore her because she is so down-to-earth and ordinary.

Life Story

Miley Cyrus is probably the biggest teen star in the USA. In *Hannah Montana* Miley got to play out a school girl's fantasy of being a pop star. In real life Miley has the hits and a new career in films, too.

Miley was raised on a farm outside Nashville Tennessee. Her father is the country singer Billy Ray Cyrus. When she was four she remembers running on stage to dance with him. Miley didn't have singing or acting lessons, but she was eager to get up and entertain. In 2001, aged eight she got her first break. She played alongside her father in the television series *Doc*. The following year she had a part in Tim Burton's film *Big Fish*. When she was 13 she got the lead in *Hannah Montana*.

Miley performs at the Rock in Rio Concert in Lisbon in 2010.

Questions and Answers

Q Where do you get your inspiration for the songs you write?

A "Just from the different things that happen in my life and different situations and stories that I hear about. Mostly. Not all my songs are love songs. I have a song about the environment and different types of things, things that are important to me. If I was my audience, if I was listening, I would want to think about what I want to hear and what I needed to hear."

Q What's the best thing about being famous?

A "The best thing I think is that I'm young but I have got to experience a lot and I love to travel and meet so many interesting people and I'm also still in school, so instead of hearing about all these places like Rome and Madrid and the UK I get to go there. I think that's pretty cool."

Miley Cyrus, *Indie London*, 2009 (both quotes)

In 2010 after four series of *Hannah Montana*, Miley stepped down from the part. The big question was could Miley make the leap from child star to serious actress and singer? The 2010 romantic film *The Last Song* was a commercial success. Now Miley has temporarily put her music career on hold so she can concentrate on being an actress. She's out to show the world that there is more to Miley than being Hannah Montana.

OTHER POP STARS

Calvin Harris

Career

Background: Calvin got into mixing demos on his big brother's computer when he was 14. Worked at a fish factory and later stacked shelves at Marks and Spencer. Signed to Sony Music and EMI Music Publishing in 2006 after he put his music on MySpace. The singing, song-writing DJ calls his music dance music.

Hits: Calvins's second album *Ready for the Weekend* (2009) was number one in the UK. In 2008 he scored two number one hit singles with *Dance Wiv Me* (with Dizzee Rascal) and *I'm Not Alone*.

Career highs: He's worked with some of the top acts in the music business including Kylie Minogue, Dizzee Rascal, JLS and Tiesto.

Favourite music: It all began with a love of Nirvana. Then he got into bass lines and 80s music. Likes the Spin Doctors.

Hobbies: Making music. If he's stressed out he gets in the car, turns up the music and drives to the country.

Website: www.calvinharris.co.uk

Basic Information

Home: Born in Dumfries, Scotland. Lives in Dumfries, Scotland.

Birthday: 17 January 1984

Cheryl Cole

Career

Background: Cheryl left school without any qualifications but wanted to be a pop star. She was working as a waitress when she auditioned for *Pop Stars: The Rivals* in 2002. She was the first to be chosen for the group Girls Aloud. In 2009 she released her first solo album, *Three Words*.

Hits: Girls Aloud's debut single *Sound of the Underground* reached number one in the UK charts. Twenty of their singles have been top-ten hits. In 2009 Cheryl's first solo single *Fight for This Love* was another number one.

Career highs: Cheryl's career is on an all-time high since she became a judge on *The X-Factor*. She's been called the 'nation's new sweetheart'. She looks set to conquer the USA with Simon Cowell at her side.

Favourite music: Whitney Houston, Sinead O'Connor, Rihanna, Snow Patrol.

Hobbies: Dancing, horse-riding and fashion.

Website: www.cherylcole.com

Basic Information

Home: Born in Newcastle, England. Lives in Surrey, England.

Birthday: 30 June 1983

Usher

Career

Background: Usher began singing in a church youth choir in Tennessee. At 13 he entered a TV talent show and was later signed to the LaFace record label. He was still at school when his debut album *Usher* (1994) was released. He is the first singer to have number one hits in the UK and USA in the 1990s, 2000s and 2010s.

Hits: In the UK Usher has had 11 top-ten singles and number one hits with *You Make Me Wanna* (1997), *Yeah* (2004), *Burn* (2004) and *OMG* (2010).

Career highs: Usher has shared a stage with Michael Jackson, Beyoncé and James Brown.

Favourite music: Al Green, Frankie Beverly, Prince, Boyz II Men, Bobby Brown and Michael Jackson.

Hobbies: Dancing, working out, fashion and watching movies.

Website: www.usherworld.com

Basic Information

Home: Born in Dallas, Texas, USA. Lives in Atlanta, Georgia.

Birthday: 14 October 1978

Taylor Swift

Career

Background: Taylor began writing songs when she was ten and picked up the guitar when she was 12. Song writing helped her get through difficult school years. The country pop singer is also an actress.

Hits: *Love Story* was a top-ten single in the USA and the UK in 2008. It also holds the record as the country song with the most paid downloads ever.

Career highs: To date Taylor has released three albums: *Taylor Swift* (2006), *Fearless* (2008) and *Speak Now* (2010). *Fearless* was a number one in the USA and reached number 5 in the UK. It was also the best-selling US album of 2009. In 2010 she picked up four Grammy Awards.

Favourite music: Shania Twain, Dolly Parton, Tina Turner and the Dixie Chicks.

Hobbies: Baking cakes, writing poetry and songs. Launching her own greeting cards.

Website: www.taylorswift.com

Basic Information

Home: Born in Wyomissing, Pennsylvania, USA. Lives in Nashville, Tennessee, USA.

Birthday: 13 December 1989

Paolo Nutini

Career

Background: Paolo's grandfather and a schoolteacher were the ones who got him into singing. For a while, Paolo looked set to work in the family fish and chip shop. At 17 he moved to London to pursue his dream of becoming a singer. He made his first demo at 18 and in 2005 was signed to Atlantic Records. Paolo sings everything from reggae and ska (mixture of calypso and jazz) to acoustic love ballads.

Hits: The single *Last Request* (2006) reached number five in the UK. His debut album *These Streets* (2006) got to number three in the UK. *Sunny Side Up* (2009) was a number one.

Career highs: Paolo Nutini gigs sell out quick. The young Scot is famous for his fantastic live performances. He's also supported some of the best acts in the business including the Rolling Stones and Ben E King.

Favourite music: Paolo loves music and that includes everything from opera, 90s dance music, reggae, Disney soundtracks to the blues. Heroes include Rodriguez, Neil Young and Bob Marley.

Hobbies: Reading, fencing and playing Football Manager on the computer.

Website: www.paolonutini.com

Basic Information

Home: Born in Paisley, Scotland. Lives in Paisley, Scotland.

Birthday: 9 January 1987

Leona Lewis

Career

Background: British R'n'B singer Leona attended Sylvia Young Theatre School, Italia Conti Academy and the BRIT School. She was working as a receptionist when she auditioned for *The X Factor*. In December 2006 she won the final and scooped a £1 million recording contract with Simon Cowell's record label Syco.

Hits: *A Moment Like This* (2006), *Bleeding Love* (2007) and *Run* (2008) were all UK chart toppers. Albums *Spirit* (2007) and *Echo* (2009) both reached the top.

Career highs: In 2006 Leona set the record for the fastest-selling UK single. Her first single *A Moment Like This* was downloaded 500,000 times within 30 minutes of being released. In 2007 Leona became the first British woman to top the US charts in over 20 years with her hit *Bleeding Heart*.

Favourite music: Mariah Carey, Celine Dion, Minnie Riperton, Whitney Houston, Eva Cassidy and Stevie Wonder.

Hobbies: Playing the piano and guitar, belly dancing.

Website: www.leonalewismusic.co.uk

Basic Information

Home: Born in London, England. Lives in London, England.

Birthday: 3 April 1985

More stars to look out for

Alexandra Burke   Ke$ha
Olly Murs   Tinchy Stryder
Katy Perry   Alicia Keys
Ellie Goulding   Kelly Rowland
Taio Cruz   Rumer

Index

acting 13, 17, 21
Akon 5
Allen, Lily 7

Beyoncé 12-13, 18, 22
Billboard Hot 100 10

Cole, Cheryl 22
Cowell, Simon 22, 23
Cyrus, Miley 20-21

Def Jam Records 5, 9
Derülo, Justin 14-15
Destiny's Child 12, 13
Dizzee Rascal 6-7, 22

fashion 5, 8, 12, 19
Fergie 4

Girls Aloud 22
Glastonbury Festival 5, 7, 19
Grammy Awards 4, 13, 18, 23

Hannah Montana 20, 21
Harris, Calvin 22

Jay-Z 9, 12, 18-19

Lady Gaga 4-5
Lewis, Leona 23
Lott, Pixie 16-17

Madonna 4
Mercury Prize 6
Mercury Records 17

NME Awards 4, 6
Nutini, Paolo 23

Obama, Barack 10, 12, 18

Queen 4

Rihanna 8-9, 22

Spears, Britney 4
Swift, Taylor 23

The X-Factor 5, 22, 23
Timberlake, Justin 4
touring 4, 5, 11, 14
Twitter 11

university 5
Usher 11, 22

YouTube 11